J B Alcott
Fromowitz, Lori
Louisa May Alcott

Louisa May Alcott

by Lori Fromowitz

Content Consultant
Adam Bradford Ph.D.

CORE
LIBRARY

Published by ABDO Publishing Company, PO Box 398166, Minneapolis, MN 55439. Copyright © 2013 by Abdo Consulting Group, Inc. International copyrights reserved in all countries. No part of this book may be reproduced in any form without written permission from the publisher. The Core Library™ is a trademark and logo of ABDO Publishing Company.

Printed in the United States of America,
North Mankato, Minnesota
112012
012013

Editor: Kari Cornell
Series Designer: Becky Daum

Cataloging-in-Publication Data
Fromowitz, Lori.
  Louisa May Alcott / Lori Fromowitz.
    p. cm. -- (Great American authors)
Includes bibliographical references and index.
ISBN 978-1-61783-715-9
1. Alcott, Louisa May, 1832–1888--Juvenile literature. 2. Authors, American--19th century--Biography--Juvenile literature. 3. Women authors, American--19th century--Biography--Juvenile literature. I. Title.
813/.4--dc23
                                        2012946797

CONTENTS

CHAPTER ONE

The Vow

"I will do something, by and by. Don't care what, teach, sew, act, write, anything to help the family; and I'll be rich and famous and happy before I die, see if I won't," cried 15-year-old Louisa May Alcott.

Louisa had just run up a hill in Concord, Massachusetts. She now sat in the spot where she often came to write, contemplating her future. Only a

The village center in Concord, Massachusetts, was surrounded by rolling hills and pretty countryside.

Concord: An Author Community

In the 1800s, Ralph Waldo Emerson asked some of his literary friends to join him in the rural town he loved. Authors such as Nathanial Hawthorne and Henry David Thoreau eventually made the community a center of literary and intellectual thought. Emerson considered Louisa's father, Bronson, a great educational reformer and thinker and asked him to move the Alcotts to Concord.

single crow was there to hear Louisa's words. But it didn't matter. She was determined in her vow to be successful and to help support her family, which was very poor. Louisa's father, Bronson, had once been a respected teacher, but now he was unable to earn any money.

At least in Concord, Bronson could grow food on the beautiful farmland. Louisa and her three sisters, Anna, Elizabeth, and May, appreciated the beauty of the New England countryside. Louisa loved to run, and her parents allowed her to roam free through the fields. In the mid-1800s, running free was not something respectable young ladies were encouraged to do. But

Ralph Waldo Emerson, a writer and poet, was a good friend of the Alcott family.

Louisa's parents had a different view of children than did many of the other parents in New England.

Concord was a special place at this time. The town was surrounded by beautiful countryside. And the people who lived there were special too. The Alcott family may have been poor, but they were surrounded by good neighbors. Some of these friends, such as Ralph Waldo Emerson and Henry

The Alcotts lived in many places while in Boston. This apartment building on Pinckney Street in the Beacon Hill neighborhood was the family's home for a time.

David Thoreau, are still thought to be some of the best American thinkers and writers.

Boston

Louisa's family had to leave Concord to earn money. Her mother, Abba, had a new social-work job in Boston, where the family had lived when Louisa was

Year	Population
1840	93,000
1850	137,000
1867	200,000
1876	341,000

Population of Boston, 1840–1876
Louisa would spend much of her adult life in Boston, even while her family had other homes. The city had seen much growth since she had first lived there as a two-year-old girl. Can you think of any ways that events discussed throughout the text may have brought about the population changes shown in the graph?

a young girl. It was a good job for Abba, who liked to help other people. The family desperately needed the money. This was not the first or last time the Alcotts had to move. They would move approximately 30 times throughout Louisa's life!

The Alcotts moved to a basement apartment in Boston, and Abba became one of the first American social workers. Her job was to help give food and advice to poor immigrants. Many of the people she helped had left Ireland after the Great Potato Famine. Louisa's family also lived through some very hard

Boston Residents

In the mid-1800s, many of Boston's residents were very poor. Many of those who lived in the city had come from Ireland to escape the Great Potato Famine. At home in Ireland, they did not have enough to eat because the potatoes they had planted didn't grow. But in Boston they continued to suffer poverty and even illness.

times in Boston, but they stuck together.

The Alcotts still had prominent friends, but life in Boston was hard work and often very difficult for the family. Louisa kept the promise she had made in Concord. While still a young woman, Louisa worked as a seamstress, companion, teacher, and actress to help support her family. Bronson gave talks about education and worked as a librarian. Still, the family struggled and often did not have enough to eat.

A New Direction

By the age of 21, Louisa had found another way to earn money. She had begun to sell her writing. She often sold her stories to magazines. She eventually

This photo of a young Alcott was taken in about 1860, when she was 28 years old.

wrote books, mostly for adults. But this was still a life of constant work, and Louisa could not make her family's worries disappear completely. That would take something completely different.

CHAPTER TWO

Topsy-Turvy Louisa

Louisa May Alcott was born on November 29, 1832, in Germantown, Pennsylvania. She was the second of four Alcott daughters and a part of a very close family. "Louy" was like her mother, one of the Fighting Mays. The Mays were a well-to-do family who had fought in the American Revolution. From early on, the Alcott family could see Louisa

Louisa's character of Jo in *Little Women* was based on Louisa herself. This illustration by Charles Edmund Brock, called "Jo's First Story," appeared in the book.

was an intelligent and energetic child. She could also be awfully stubborn!

When Louisa was two years old, her family moved to Boston, where Bronson ran Temple School. This school became well known because of Bronson's unique ideas about children. Bronson believed children should be valued for their ideas. He encouraged his students to think and study the world around them. In other schools in the 1830s, students were expected to sit still and memorize facts. Bronson also believed that teachers should not hit their students. This was an unusual belief at the time.

Amos Bronson Alcott relaxes on a rustic seat in Concord, Massachusetts.

But some of Bronson's beliefs were too different for people in Boston. The Temple School was forced to close after a few years. The Alcotts moved to Concord, where they would spend the next several years.

The Alcott Sisters

Each of the Alcott sisters had a unique personality. Anna, the oldest sister, was ladylike and practical. Elizabeth, who was called Lizzie, was the third sister. She was "the angel in the house." Lizzie had a sweet temperament. She was interested in domestic life and music. May, the youngest sister, liked fine things. She was the artist, and her family encouraged her to draw.

Louisa was close to her three sisters, but she was different from them too. She didn't care much for girl's things. She wasn't known for her ladylike manners, either. She liked to climb trees and leap fences. Bronson and Abba worried about their wild daughter.

Louisa's sister May drew this sketch of Jo and Beth for Louisa's book *Little Women*.

Louisa, the Writer

As a teenager in Concord, Louisa wrote melodramas that she and her sisters performed for family and friends. From a very young age, Louisa also wrote poetry and kept a journal. In Boston, Louisa continued to write, while struggling at many jobs. At 17, Louisa wrote her first novel, *The Inheritance.*

When Louisa was 22, her first book was published. *Flower Fables* was a book of fairy stories she wrote for Emerson's daughter. "My book came out," wrote Louisa, "and people began to think that

Louisa's Education

Louisa did not attend school for most of her childhood. Instead, she was often taught by her father and his friends. One of these friends, Henry David Thoreau, became famous for his writing about living with nature. Louisa would take nature walks with Thoreau. He helped Louisa think in new ways about the world around her. Another friend, Ralph Waldo Emerson, was very generous with Louisa. He often let Louisa visit his grand library and borrow books. Louisa loved to read, and she read many books as a young girl.

topsy-turvy Louisa would amount to something after all."

A Working Writer

Louisa's growing success as a writer was very encouraging. She dreamed of helping her family, especially her exhausted mother. Louisa continued to work as a teacher. But she knew she could be a famous writer someday. She was persistent. Once, an important editor did not like a story Louisa wrote. He told her, "Stick to your teaching."

"I can write," she told him, "and I'll prove it."

Louisa works at her writing desk in Orchard House.

FURTHER EVIDENCE

There was quite a bit of information about Louisa May Alcott and her family in Chapter Two. But if you could pick out the main point of the chapter, what would it be? Visit the Web site below to learn more about the Alcott family. Choose a quote from the Web site that relates to this chapter. Write a few sentences explaining how the quote you found relates to the chapter.

The Alcott Family

www.louisamayalcott.org/witandwisdom.html

CHAPTER THREE

Writing What She Knew

In 1856, May and Elizabeth became sick with scarlet fever. Although both sisters seemed to recover at first, Elizabeth would never again be quite well. She died two years later at the age of 22. Alcott was heartbroken. Her family was forever changed.

After Lizzie's death, the Alcotts moved into another house in Concord. Bronson was very excited

Orchard House in Concord was home to the Alcotts for almost 20 years. It was here that Alcott wrote *Little Women*.

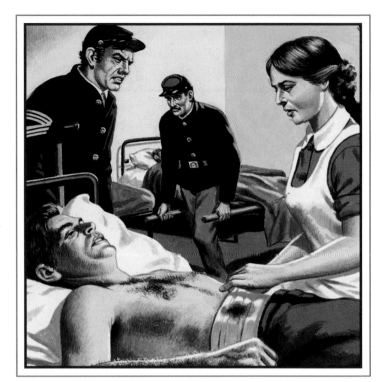

Alcott took care of many soldiers during the American Civil War.

to fix up their new home. He called it Orchard House. The Alcotts would live here for 19 years.

In 1860, Alcott received exciting news. She had tried many times to sell her stories to the well-respected *Atlantic Monthly*. Finally the magazine accepted "Love and Self-Love." Alcott began to see her dreams slowly coming true. That year, the Alcotts had another big family change. Anna married her sweetheart, John Pratt, at Orchard House.

Louisa Goes to War

In 1861 the American Civil War broke out. The Alcotts hated slavery. They did what they could to support the Union. Alcott could remember her family hiding a fugitive slave when she was a girl. But this wasn't enough. She wanted to do more. She wished she could be a soldier!

Women were not allowed to be soldiers in the 1860s, though. So Alcott signed up to be a nurse in the Union Army. "I want new experiences,"

EXPLORE ONLINE

The focus in Chapter Three is Alcott's writing and the start of her successful career. It also touched on Alcott's time as a nurse during the Civil War. The Web Site below focuses on hospitals during the Civil War. As you know, every source is different. How is the information given on the Web site different from the information in this chapter? What can you learn from this Web site?

Civil War Hospitals
www.kidport.com/reflib/usahistory/CivilWar/Hospitals/.htm

said Alcott, "and I am sure to get 'em if I go." In 1862, Alcott went to Washington DC to serve in a hospital. Alcott made friends with many patients in the hospital. She described her experiences at the hospital in letters home.

Typhoid Fever

It was easy for disease to spread in the hospital. After only a short time, Alcott caught typhoid fever. Alcott was treated with medicine that contained mercury. Doctors thought this helped people with typhoid fever. They didn't realize mercury is poison! Alcott would recover from the typhoid fever, but she would never again be the healthy woman she was before the war.

A Serious Author

After Alcott returned home, the editors of a weekly newspaper had an idea for her. They wanted her to publish the letters she had written home from the hospital. They were published in serialization in the weekly and then as a book. *Hospital Sketches* was not all fact, but the book gave readers a picture of what life was like for the

Illness	Infected Soldiers
Typhoid Fever	79,462
Yellow Fever	50,061
Measles	76,318
Mumps	60,314

Illnesses Contracted by Union Troops During the Civil War

Soldiers suffered from more than just battle wounds. How does this chart add to the information about Civil War illness and medical care shown in the text?

hospital's soldiers. This was Alcott's first successful book. Finally, she was earning respect as a writer like her old friends Emerson and Thoreau.

Alcott next wrote *Moods*, a novel for adults. The book talked about divorce, a daring topic for the time. She was excited about the book, but it did not turn out as she hoped. She felt too many changes had been made by the publisher, and it was no longer a good story. *Moods* was not as well liked by readers as was *Hospital Sketches*.

Alcott spent much of her time writing, but she also loved to read.

Another Name

Over the next few years, Alcott continued to sell her stories to magazines. She had also started to write different kinds of stories. Alcott had a talent for writing creative and dark thrillers for adults. She earned a good living from these stories. But they were not the stories she wanted people to think of when they heard her name. Alcott used the name A.M. Barnard for these tales so readers would not know who wrote them!

A Girls' Book

In 1867, Alcott was working as the editor of *Merry's Museum*, a children's magazine. At the same time, a book publisher named Thomas Niles asked Alcott if she would write a girls' book.

Alcott thought this was a bad idea. She had never cared for girls' things as a child. But Alcott still had a family to support. How could she say no?

Now 35 years old, Alcott was living at Orchard House. There was one group of girls she remembered well. Maybe people would be interested in the stories of the Alcott sisters growing up in Concord. Alcott started to write about her memories. She wrote without stopping. Part I of *Little Women* was finished in only ten weeks!

She set her book at Orchard House during the Civil War. Although the novel was fiction, much of it was inspired by Alcott's life and the memories of her sisters and Abba. The March sisters in *Little Women* all had personalities much like Alcott and her

Little Women

"We really lived most of it," wrote Alcott about *Little Women*. "And if it succeeds that will be the reason of it." She was right. The March girls, like the Alcott sisters, were not perfect. This is what made them seem real to readers. Alcott joined her imagination with her real-life experiences. Had Alcott been a little less rebellious and a little more ladylike, her much-loved character, Jo March, would never have come to be.

three sisters. The main character, Josephine, or "Jo," was rebellious, intelligent, and a little wild—just like Alcott!

Success at Last

When *Little Women* was first published at the end of 1868, it was an instant best seller. It sold so many copies that more had to be ordered right away.

Alcott's readers insisted on another book. Children wanted to see how the story ended for the March girls! They wanted to know whom the girls married. Alcott had never married herself. She thought it was important for girls to know that marriage did not have to be a woman's only goal.

In this 1948 illustration by Salomon Van Abbe from *Little Women*, Jo wins the game of croquet with a clever stroke.

This woodcut illustration appeared in an early edition of Alcott's book, *Little Women*.

She tried to show this view in the second book, *Good Wives*, and in the books she wrote later.

Thanks to the success of *Little Women* and *Good Wives*, Alcott was now a wealthy woman. She was finally able to pay off all of her family's debts. Alcott would be one of the most successful authors of her time.

This excerpt from Chapter Six of *Little Women* focuses on Beth March and the big house.

> *The big house did prove a Palace Beautiful, though it took some time for all to get in, and Beth found it very hard to pass the lions. Old Mr. Laurence was the biggest one, but after he had called, said something funny or kind to each one of the girls, and talked over old times with their mother, nobody felt much afraid of him, except timid Beth. The other lion was the fact that they were poor and Laurie rich: for this made them shy of accepting favors which they could not return. But, after a while, they found that he considered them the benefactors, and could not do enough to show how grateful he was for Mrs. March's motherly welcome, their cheerful society, and the comfort he took in that humble home of theirs.*

Alcott, Louisa May. Little Women. University Press: John Wilson & Sons, Cambridge, 1880.

What's the Big Idea?

Carefully read this passage from Alcott's *Little Women*. Determine the main idea of the text and explain how the main idea is supported by details. Be sure to discuss at least two or three supporting details.

"Louise Alcott"
The Children's Friend.

Lizbeth B. Comins

CHAPTER FOUR

The Writing Life

In 1870, after Alcott had published *Good Wives*, she and May took a trip to Europe. They had a wonderful time and enjoyed a much-needed rest. But while they were away, the sisters learned their brother-in-law, John Pratt, had died. Alcott wanted to do something to help her two young nephews. She went to work on *Little Men* right away. She gave all the money she earned from this book to her nephews.

Alcott was famous for the stories she wrote for children. Here she reads *Little Women* to a captive audience.

May loved to draw as much as her sister loved to write. May drew this sketch of a mother with her child on her bedroom door at Orchard House.

In the book *Little Men*, Jo March is now married to Professor Bhaer. Together, they run a school for boys called Plumfield. Once again, Alcott used her own experiences to inspire her stories. Children were unknowingly learning about Bronson's ideas about education.

A Natural Source of Stories

Alcott was now as wealthy and successful as she had always hoped. Yet she couldn't stop writing. She sometimes wrote to the point of exhaustion.

Alcott continued to be best known for her children's works, such as *Eight Cousins* and its sequel, *Rose in Bloom*. She was able to earn a good living from her children's stories. Her books often had strong female characters. Some of these women earned their own livings and made their own way, which wasn't easy in the 1800s. But Alcott thought if she could do it, so could her characters.

Alcott didn't want to write only for children. She wanted to be known for her adult books too.

More Books

Alcott wrote her next book, *An Old-Fashioned Girl*, right after *Good Wives* was published. The story follows an independent music teacher named Polly. Polly teaches her friends that kindness and good deeds matter more than wealth. Like many works of the time, it was published in individual chapters in a magazine before becoming a book.

CHAPTER FIVE

Keeping a Promise

The busy Alcott continued to write and support her family. When Abba died in 1877, Alcott could be happy knowing that her hardworking mother had finally lived a life of comfort.

Alcott had used some of her money to make sure May would study art in Europe. May now enjoyed life as a respected artist. In Europe, May also fell in love and got married. Sadly, she died shortly after giving

This woodcut shows Alcott in her later years.

birth to her first child, Louisa May. She asked for her daughter to be sent to America to live with the aunt after whom she was named. Alcott spent many of the last years of her life taking care of her niece, "Lulu."

Alcott had often been ill since coming down with typhoid fever. She died on March 6, 1888, only two days after her father. As she had sworn at the age of 15, she had lived to support her family and had become a successful writer.

Louisa Lives On

Alcott had always thought that to be remembered as a great author, she would need to be known as more than just a writer for children. If she were alive today, Alcott would probably be surprised to hear of some of the important writers she inspired with her children's work. These authors include Cynthia Ozick, Ursula Le Guin, Gertrude Stein, JK Rowling, Nora Ephron, and many more.

There's one more thing that would probably be a surprise to Alcott. Nearly 150 years after *Little Women* was first published, it is still so popular that she would be able to buy it in a bookstore!

Alcott's Work Today

Little Women and *Good Wives* are now published as one book, called *Little Women* Part I and II. It is still the most popular of Alcott's works. Each year, tens of thousands of visitors from all over the world visit Orchard House to see the home where Alcott wrote *Little Women*.

On a tour of Orchard House, Alcott fans can see her bedroom and the half-circle desk where she wrote *Little Women*.

This excerpt from *Hospital Sketches* focuses on Alcott's experience as a nurse.

> *More flattering than the most gracefully turned compliment, more grateful than the most admiring glance, was the sight of those rows of faces, all strange to me a little while ago, now lighting up, with smiles of welcome, as I came among them, enjoying that moment heartily, with a womanly pride in their regard, a motherly affection for them all. The evenings were spent in reading aloud, writing letters, waiting on and amusing the men, going the rounds with Dr. P., as he made his second daily survey, dressing my dozen wounds afresh, giving last doses, and making them cozy for the long hours to come, till the nine o'clock bell rang, the gas was turned down, the day nurses went off duty, the night watch came on, and my nocturnal adventure began.*

Alcott, Louisa May. Hospital Sketches. Boston: James Redpath, 1863.

Nice View

Re-read the excerpt on page 31 and this excerpt again. Think about Alcott's point of view in each. Is it different? Write a short essay that answers: What is the point of view of Alcott in each excerpt? How is it similar and why? How is it different and why?

IMPORTANT DATES

November 29, 1832
Louisa May Alcott is born.

September 1834
Bronson Alcott opens Temple School in Boston.

March 23, 1839
The Alcott family moves to Concord.

December 1854
Louisa's first book, *Flower Fables*, is published.

March 14, 1858
Elizabeth Alcott, Louisa's sister, dies.

April 7, 1858
The Alcotts purchase Orchard House and live there for 19 years.

August 1863
Hospital Sketches, based on Alcott's experiences as an army nurse, is published.

December 1868
Little Women is published.

April 1869
Good Wives (*Little Women* Part 2) is published.

July 1870
An Old-Fashioned Girl is published as a book.

May 1871
Little Men is published. Alcott gives the proceeds to sister Anna's children.

March 6, 1888
Louisa May Alcott dies.

KEY WORKS

Eight Cousins

This children's novel tells the story of the orphan Rose and her seven male cousins.

Alcott, Louisa May. *Eight Cousins*. Boston: Roberts Brothers, 1875. Print.

Flower Fables

Louisa's first published book was originally made up from tales she wrote for Ralph Waldo Emerson's daughter.

Alcott, Louisa May. *Flower Fables*. Boston: George W. Briggs and Co, 1855. Print.

Hospital Sketches

This book of scenes is based on Louisa's experiences as a nurse in the Union Army during the American Civil War.

Alcott, Louisa May. *Hospital Sketches*. Boston: James Redpath, 1863. Print.

The Inheritance

Written when Louisa was 17, this book was not published until almost 150 years later.

Alcott, Louisa May. *The Inheritance*. Edited by Joel Myerson and Daniel Shealy. New York: Penguin Putnam, 1997. Print.

Little Men

A sequel to Little Women, this book focuses on Jo and Professor Bhaer's school for boys at Plumfield.

Alcott, Louisa May. *Little Men*. Boston: Roberts Brothers, 1871. Print.

Little Women

Louisa's semi-autobiographical book about the four March sisters is her most famous work.

Alcott, Louisa May. *Little Women*. Boston: Roberts Brothers, 1868. Print.

Moods

One of Louisa's favorite works, it was not popular at first. She rewrote it later in her life.

Alcott, Louisa May. *Moods*. Loring, 1865. Print.

An Old-Fashioned Girl

Polly teaches her friends about the importance of good deeds over wealth.

Alcott, Louisa May. *An Old-Fashioned Girl*. Boston: Roberts Brothers, 1869. Print.

Why Do I Care?

Louisa May Alcott used stories from her own memories to write *Little Women* and some of her other books. The books are fiction, but they are inspired by real events that she experienced or saw. Have you ever wanted to write a story about something that has happened to you, your family, or your friends? What stories would you use? Would you change them? Why?

Changing Minds

This book discusses Louisa May Alcott's decision to join the Union Army as a nurse and both the illness and literary success that followed. Do you think she would have made the same decision if she had known what the results of her choice would be? Take a position on her decision and write a short essay detailing your opinion, reasons for your opinion, and details that support those reasons.

Surprise Me

Think about what you learned from this book. Can you name the two or three facts in this book that you found most surprising? Write a short paragraph about each, describing what you found surprising and why.

Tell the Tale

In this book, you learned that Louisa May Alcott wrote melodramas and performed them with her sisters. With an adult's help, research what makes a melodrama. Write 200 words that use a melodramatic plot and characters. Be sure to set the scene, develop a sequence of events, and offer a conclusion.

GLOSSARY

contemplating
thinking about or considering

domestic
relating to the home

encouraging
positive; giving hope

inspired
based on an idea, came from

melodrama
a play with an exaggerated dramatic plot featuring a hero, heroine, and villain

persistent
not stopping; determined to succeed; stubborn

practical
reasonable and sensible purpose

rebellious
stubborn, not following the rules

serialization
a larger work published in pieces over time

vow
solemn promise

LEARN MORE

Books

Gormley, Beatrice. *Louisa May Alcott: Young Novelist*. New York: Aladdin Paperbacks, 1999. Print.

Whelan, Gloria. *Fruitlands: Louisa May Alcott Made Perfect*. New York: HarperCollins, 2004. Print.

Zeldis McDonough, Yona, and Bethanne Andersen. *Louisa: The Life of Louisa May Alcott*. New York: Henry Holt and Co, 2009. Print.

Web Links

To learn more about Louisa May Alcott, visit ABDO Publishing Company online at **www.abdopublishing.com**. Web sites about Louisa May Alcott are featured on our Book Links page. These links are routinely monitored and updated to provide the most current information available. Visit **www.mycorelibrary.com** for free additional tools for teachers and students.

INDEX

ABOUT THE AUTHOR

Lori Fromowitz is a freelance writer and editor. She graduated from Bard College, where she studied theater and playwriting. Lori is currently pursuing a master's degree. She lives in Somerville, Massachusetts.